IMAGE OF ABSENCE
[LEVE SANGRE]

IMAGE OF ABSENCE
[LEVE SANGRE]

Jeannette L. Clariond

TRANSLATED BY
Curtis Bauer

INTERNATIONAL EDITIONS
Barbara Goldberg, Series Editor
THE WORD WORKS
WASHINGTON, D.C.

Image of Absence copyright © 2018 Curtis Bauer

Reproduction of any part of this book in any form or by any means, electronic or mechanical, except when quoted in part for the purpose of review, must be with permission in writing from the publisher.
Address inquiries to:
The Word Works
P.O. Box 42164
Washington, D.C. 20015
editor@wordworksbooks.org

Cover art: Bronlyn Jones
Author photograph: Mauricio de la Garza
Translator photograph: Idoia Elola
Cover design: Susan Pearce

LCCN: 2018931395
ISBN: 978-1-944585-22-8

Acknowledgments

The translator gratefully acknowledges the following journals and magazines in which some of these translations first appeared (sometimes in different incarnations), and thanks their editors for their generous support of this work and of poetry in translation in general.

The Southern Review: "Your voice reached like a ladder,"
   "After my death," "No one says anything," &
   "Not everything is what is said"

Shadowgraph: "Lost, I watched the afternoon"

Also, profound gratitude is given to the kind patrons at Residencia Roquissar in Valldemossa Spain who provided uninterrupted time and beautiful spaces to work on this book; and to the Vermont Studio Center for the translation fellowships that allowed the author and translator the valuable time and space to collaborate and complete this project, in particular Ryan Walsh and Gary Clark.

I would like to express more gratitude to my colleagues in the Creative Writing and Comparative Literatures programs, the Department of English, and Department of Classical and Modern Languages and Literatures at Texas Tech University, in particular Carmen Pereira-Muro, Idoia Elola, Susan Larson, Don Lavigne, and David Larmour for their assistance with particular Spanish, Latin, and Italian usages in this collection, and to Christopher Witmore for introducing me to the term "ground-truthing"; to John Poch, Jessica Smith, and Chen Chen for their comments on the manuscript; and to Bruce Clarke and Brian Still for their administrative kindness while I worked to complete this collection. Thanks to the Lubbock Scapes Collective for creating generous and invigorating intellectual and creative space to try out these translations. Thank you to The Word Works, Nancy White, and Barbara Goldberg for believing in this project, for their endless patience with me and my drafts and questions and for welcoming me into The Word Works family.

Thank you Mira Rosenthal, Aviya Kushner, Patrick Rosal, Ross Gay, Carl Adamshick, and Susan Steinberg, generous poets, translators, readers, and friends who have helped me refine this book, the introduction, and title: your grace. Thank you to Jean Valentine, Don Bogen, Rebecca Gayle Howell, and Christopher Merrill for such close, bighearted readings of this work; without your encouragement I'm not sure this book would be what it is now.

I am privileged to have received such a rigorous education in Spanish language, literature, and culture from so many, in particular my family in Spain, Mexico, and Argentina. Thanks always to the Basque for her patience.

Finally, my deepest gratitude to Jeannette Clariond for trusting me with her poems, these beautiful, difficult, and important poems. I am honored.

Contents

Preface ... 9
Translator's Introduction ... 11

I.   LA TARDE / DUSK ... 17

II.   RECORDACIÓN / REMINISCENCE ... 29

III.   EL ORDEN DEL MUNDO /
THE ORDER OF THE WORLD ... 41

IV.   SOMOS LA HERIDA / WE ARE THE WOUND ... 69

V.   UN ALTAR LA AUSENCIA /
AN ALTAR OF ABSENCE ... 79

VI.   NUESTRA DESCREENCIA /
OUR DISBELIEF ... 101

MYSTERIUM TERRAE ... 117

Notes ... 129
About the Author / About the Translator ... 133
The Word Works / Other Word Works Books ... 134

Preface

Mexican poet Jeanette Clariond takes us on a daring journey—metaphysical, not physical; philosophical, not rational. She is seeking the path to the dark recesses of her soul. Like mystics before her, she is traveling solo. No signposts. No guides.

Her way forward requires her to fully immerse herself in silence and absence—two all-consuming forces with whom she must become intimate. One cannot come to terms with the human condition without being inside the beating heart of absence and silence.

A stone is silent, but its silence has resonance:

> *The stone burns in its solitude.*
> Stone that I let die on my path
> —I too was a stone—
>   silence like the beginning of its resonance.

And absence is a presence to be reckoned with. "The Book says: create the single image of reality. / I say: create the image of absence."

Clariond isn't troubled by paradox—the resonance of silence, the image of absence. Indeed, she courts paradox as being emblematic of a greater truth—a sun that both soothes and parches. Poems are born in silence. "There is nothing certain in the sky. / Nothing. Not even these words."

But then she embarks on a glorious display of lush and lyrical language: "Perhaps that cluster of gardenias beside the cypress, / the red horizon when the end opens."

For someone who extols silence, she shows again and again her mastery with words: "That evening I went back to the lagoon. An immense solitude looked / at me. I saw the desert bird sink into the horizon, the sun fall over / the cedars, the shadow sink into me."

Here the text is ecstatic, even erotic. "I sink in the desire to lose myself, / in the lake that shifts me about: / being, where does my being abide?" Clariond "sinks" into an eroticism that is not housed in the flesh: "I eroticize what I touch / Except for flesh / My desire is so great."

The human element in Clariond's work plays only a minor role. There is someone called Liel, there is a mother, a father, a grandmother. But we don't know them with any kind of specificity. Perhaps she is saying that it doesn't matter. Each absence is an abandonment; each silence, an echo.

If she surrenders to anything, it is to God. But her God "will find refuge in *my* (emphasis mine) prayers." God seems to dwell inside Clariond's devotion and offers refuge amidst the swirling tempest of sound and presence.

Barbara Goldberg
Washington, D.C.

Translator's Introduction

In 2010, shortly before the Spanish press Pre-Textos published Jeannette Clariond's book *Leve Sangre*, I made the reckless decision—reckless because the text was so difficult and mysterious—to teach the first three sections of this book to a translation seminar at Texas Tech University. Jeannette and I had met through mutual friends a few years before, and I had found some money to pay for her trip and a slight honorarium for her to give a talk and reading. Days before her arrival I started reading my students' work: I knew I would receive terrible teaching evaluations that semester; they had failed to capture the complex textures of her poems—the rich sound, dense allusions, the archaic Spanish and the mixture of Latin and Italian poems woven into her own, to name only a few of the complications; I would have to help them. We shared our attempts with Jeannette when she visited the university, and it was clear that we all had failed miserably on that project. However, we had beautiful arguments about her voice, the trajectory of the poems and the seemingly impossible task of how to translate absence, as well as the many sensations absence imprints upon one's body and psyche.

By then I had fallen in love with the poems in this collection; they are so unlike any poems I can imagine writing. Clariond is considerably more experimental than other writers I have translated. Her fragment use has a logic not immediately apparent, her allusions are obscure and far-reaching, she varies how she uses space across pages, and her own Italian and Latin verses materialize like some Gregorian chant out of the atmospheres she creates through multiple voices, appeals to God, and unnamed or obscure mythical figures. These elements, as well as sudden shifts of focus and challenging syntactical structures, make her work challenging for the translator and also for readers. Her poems are obscure in Spanish—she does not include endnotes—and this, therefore, raises the question of how to represent that obscurity in English translation. My response has been to operate somewhat more freely than in other translations I have done, attempting to focus on larger conceptual nuances, rather than precise meanings. I often felt the need to "clarify" or "explain" many of Clariond's gestures, but that feeling was like a magnet repelling its likeness, directing me instead to reveal the musical depths, the importance of silence inside these poems in order to capture—*to expose*—absence and accentuate their lyric resonances. I should note that the poet considers *Leve Sangre* a single poem in seven sections, and for that reason I have maintained the section breaks as indications of the shifts of voice and tone within the whole poem. However, I also believe it is possible to read this book as a collection of distinct poems, and therefore to discuss them as such throughout this introduction.

The title *Leve Sangre* highlights two fundamental aspects: *light*, remote, the elaboration of an essential poetic; and *blood*, the vital, the spiritual. This title was a growing cause of anxiety while translating this collection. If I were to offer a literal translation, perhaps it wouldn't be so problematic. Blood and its weight; however, these concepts do not properly convey the complex attributes of loss, of suffering, of uncertainty this book embodies. Light: brief. Blood: red, but red like *rubedo*, a Latin word meaning "redness," signaling alchemical success and the end of the great work. *Rubedo* is also known by the Greek word, *Iosis*. Red is fervor, in it an allusion—for Clariond—to the mysticism about love for the 11th century Persian poet Ruzbehan Baqli. Poetry and devotion. At first glance one might see echoes of Anne Carson and Alda Merini, two poets she has translated and therefore internalized. *Leve* and *Sangre* for Clariond also gesture toward the failure of our body in the face of great loss: blood slows, doesn't function the way it should, and our body clambers to silence, becomes an absence of what it once was, which is that vibrancy, that levity and surging force.

How to translate such complexity without favoring one idea or motion over another, and how to be concise: these are a few of the struggles translators face. I arrived at my solution—*Image of Absence*—by looking at the collection from a different angle: what is present and what is not? What are these poems, through their various and varied forms and modes of discourse, distinct voices, indicated through change of format and punctuation, what are these prose poems, single-line verses, vocatives, silences, and white spaces putting pressure on? For me they are working to create an aura of that which is no longer immediately present. To fully comprehend *Image of Absence* it may help to read the white space around the poems, attempt to read the italicized sections as different voices, and to read aloud the Latin and Italian in the context of the Spanish, and keep in mind that the poet wrote almost all of these segments that remain in Italian or Latin herself, maintaining the voice in which the poems were "spoken" to her. Yes, this sounds odd, but consider voices we always have in our heads, remnants of overheard conversations, annotations of what we have read, people we have encountered across our lives. Even when they are gone, as is the case of Clariond's close family, their breath still breathes in the language of these poems.

Because there is no clear narrative thread to follow, we must be willing to leap across lyric moments, across spaces and uncertain aspects of time. A close, slow reading—that is what this book requires—reveals an elegant musical intoning that then leads to uncover even richer levels of mineral wealth, that of the aphoristic quality, the constant movement toward an embodiment of an emotion, and the grounding of these poems, these ideas, these attempts to capture the ineffable in a much larger tradition. Formally, this is the richest and most demanding book in her full body of work. The poems in *Image of Absence* for her are spaces where myths meld with experiences, where blood's voice, that central force and energy inside us, speaks, where absence materializes. In this book various poetic forms coexist, some new to her discourse: she uses aphoristic fragments, prose poems, calligramatic or Mallarméan arrangements of the lines across the page, plays with italics, scattered arrangements, and interplaying voices.

The poems in *Image of Absence* reveal valuable fragments of insight; they uncover an architecture of relationships, emotions, memory, and perhaps most difficult of all, silence and absence; they reveal artifacts of beauty so often buried under the detritus of the noisy world we live in, or they pull out of the trash a present habitation in melancholy, which subsequently overshadows and taints our memories and experiences of the past. We forget, we become deaf and blind to nuance; these poems provide a clearer vision of resolve, placing substance where we perceive the conceptual, tuning our ear to perceive the delicate music of memory's aftermath.

If you have read Wallace Stevens, or Anne Carson, or Charles Wright, or W. S. Merwin, or Alda Merini, all poets Clariond has translated into Spanish eloquently and to much praise, you will hear echoes of their voices in hers, resonances of their poetics. For in fact, she carries different voices inside her, and they don't all speak Spanish. Hers is a language and poetry of experience, "a poetics of ancestries," one the critic Jaime Parra notes "is bound to thirst, thirst as a source, thirst as a destiny. Thirst is what orients her… thirst is a motive for life" ("Poetics of Origen," 2017, translation mine). She has learned how to refine her own particulars by gazing upon the foreign. Heir of a certain Hispano-American and North American tradition, Clariond carries forward the literary DNA of masters of constraint and elaboration like Vallejo, Paz, Williams, and Stevens. Translation for her is essential, as it was for Pound and Paz, because it allows an inhalation of otherness in her poems, an essence unlike any other poet writing in Mexico today.

Searching for a better way to describe Clariond's collection, I'm reminded of the term *ground-truthing* in the field of archeology, which is used when researchers need to compare satellite data to what is on the ground before them—the collection of ground-truth data enables archeologists to adjust what they know from afar and aids in their interpretation and analysis of what is being sensed in the moment. I have always found this term fascinating and applicable to good poetry, poems that stay with me and change the way I perceive and understand the world I inhabit. Without any knowledge of my interest in archeology, Clariond mentioned in a recent letter that she is interested in archeology, too, and that she understands poetry as the speech that rises from the ruins.

Archeologists must also consider the imprint they leave on the site where they have been working, digging. The poems in Clariond's collection indicate that serious emotional excavation has occurred, and they leave an imprint on the ground on which her readers tread.

Tomorrow, next month, next year, if we read these poems closely, we may be surprised to find the artifact of these poems' resonance remaining: shards of music in falling ash, or in a simple perception of space, revealed in koan-like truths that leave us pondering, as in: "What do we search for? What does the flame reach for in its limits? / Distance is what we can never name." Or from another poem, "I want to contemplate the monument, / the cliffs, the silver scattered on the shore. // *Of all silence, I prefer the sea.*"

Clariond's relentless investigation of memory and absence, as well as her melding of literal and figurative experience in these poems, offers the reader much to consider and appreciate. "Come, let me kiss your eyes, dawn sheds its fog in the orchard." she writes in a sequence in the third section. "Read with me the pages of an unwritten story, steps / in the snow, tender hands fading with the hours, / your words, like sand, dissolving on the dunes." And later in the same section, "That sky does not fade from my eyes. I still dream of / your steps on the stained gray granite." The reader as literary archeologist will find artifacts, remnants of her unique voice present in how we perceive the world after we put this book down.

Jeannette called me from Mexico a month before I completed this book. She wanted to make sure I understood that she is aware of how difficult her poems are, that the language she uses may seem archaic or unusual, and that I should feel at ease about my translation, that I need to "make them good poems in English," and that I shouldn't worry about loss of literal meaning. I feel fortunate to have been granted this kind of liberty, and I am deeply grateful that I have been entrusted with conveying this important book, the first translation of one of her books into English, to those who cannot read it in its original. Every translator wants this kind of permission. Her primary concern is that details, the suggested and absent details of the many voices here, be present, "even if only in the silence around the words."

Curtis Bauer
Lubbock, TX

I

LA TARDE / DUSK

Extraviada, miré la tarde contra el viento desnudo,
las hojas caídas escuché.

Vacía, Emily, ¿es real que la tarde se vacía?

La poesía, es ausencia de agua, puerta
que abre otra puerta y otra y una más.

Nada entraba en mis ojos o en mi lengua
que no fuera belleza.

Tomé un cuaderno, un lápiz afilado,
encendí una vela en plena luz.

Salí a caminar por calles oscuras,
el horizonte se abrió lento ante mis ojos.

Lost, I watched the afternoon against the naked wind,
listened to the fallen leaves.

Empty, Emily, does the afternoon really empty?

Poetry, that absence of water, a door
that opens another, another and yet another.

Nothing entered my eyes or crossed my tongue
that was not beauty.

I took out a notebook, a sharpened pencil,
lit a candle in full light.

I went out to walk the darkened streets,
the horizon opened unhurriedly before me.

Necesitaba del silencio, como la muerte el destello de la flor, madrigales para hundir mi leve sangre, piedras de río donde enjugar el paño sagrado.

    Dios optó por la parvedad; creyó que su creación había terminado con el barro y la belleza de la criatura. Ignoró la desolación, no pudo ver más allá de sus manos, lo blanco del pensamiento que asciende a las alturas con el azor.

    ¡Callad, hermanos muertos! ¡No alcéis vuestras voces,
    romperíais las vasijas!

    ¡Cubrid la podredumbre en los ojos del hambre!

… las palmeras se agitaban con el céfiro, los cristales trizaban su soledad, astillando las jarcias del árbol que me vio nacer.

    ¡Mas no lloréis vuestra falta, precipitaríais el final!
    ¡Derrumbad el altar del austero incitador de los inocentes!

    (La palma datilera atormentará
    la mesa encumbrada por los reyes).

… atados sus pies, los arrastraron por el desierto, sus cabellos envueltos en paños magenta, memoria del oscuro signo del carey.

    ¡Dilatad vuestros pasos bajo el sol, abrazaos a
    la serpiente cuyo rastro de arena es el más puro!

    ¡Bebed vuestra sed y cada quien bendiga su expresión!

    (La palabra encenderá desnudos cielos,
    órdenes para labrar los cristalinos huesos
    que asoman en la vega ramosa: pálpito
    de nuestra orfandad).

Vengan peces a mi orilla, alimenten mi salsedumbre,
mis labios beberán del vino sin reconocer la escama de su linaje.

From silence I needed, like death seeks a spark from the flower bloom, madrigals to cleanse my quiet blood, river stones
to cleanse the shroud.

> God preferred blindness; He deemed creation had ended with mud and the beauty of the created. God ignored desolation, He could not see beyond His hands, rumination's white ascending to the high spheres of the goshawk.

> *Quiet, dead brothers! Do not raise your voices; you could break the vessels!*

> *Cover the rot in hunger's eyes!*

… the palm trees shake in the gentle wind, the windows shattered their solitude, uprooting the tree that watched my birth.

> *Cry no more for your desire: the end will come soon enough!*
> *Tear down the altar of the unadorned inciter of the innocent!*

> (The date palm will insult
> the table praised by kings).

…they drug them, feet tied, through the desert, their hair wrapped in magenta cloth, the memory of the tortoise's dark spur.

> *Trudge, step beneath the sun, embrace*
> *the serpent whose gritty countenance is pure!*

> *Drink from your thirst and each be blessed with its tongue!*

> (The word will lighten naked skies,
> orders to till the crystalline bones
> that emerge on the rich, low-land
> plains: our abandonment's breath).

Come fish to my shore, nourish my brackishness, my lips will drink the wine and not comprehend the scope of its origin.

¡Un sol lastimará la mejilla que ofrecisteis pues nada es más digno de ofensa que el anhelo de la propia hiel!

(Ríes con risa sardónica, lavas tus manos en la noria lamosa con el pudor de un dios que busca borrar las manchas purpúreas del universo)

Dios, ¿por qué desgarra tu granizo las tiernas hojas de los tréboles?

Oh mar
Acoge
Mi desamparo

Y el viento anunció que nuestra sería la miseria:
Illa nec misere morietur, nec omnino morietur.

Era su sonrisa el brillo plateado en la albufera, ráfaga incrustada en mis entrañas, vuelo de ánsares su mirada por la que ascendí los montes del origen. Y sin temor me demoré en sus pupilas, penetrando sus olas.

The sun will strike the cheek you turned, though nothing dignifies the offense more than one's own bitterness!

> (You laugh scornful laughter, wash your hands at the moss-covered water-wheel with the shame of a god who wishes to wipe away the purple stains of the universe)

Lord, why does your hail destroy the innocent clover?

Oh sea
Give refuge to
My helplessness

> And the wind cried that ours would be misery:
> *Illa nec misere moriatur, nec omnino morietur.*

His smile was silver sheen on the low rock, encrusted squall in my entrails, her gaze the mallard flight on which I ascended the ancient mountains. Fearless, I lingered in his eyes, falling into his waves.

En el lento devenir de su pensamiento yo era luciérnaga, pasos en la incierta vereda.

Y el viento de mi corazón batía
vela en el vendaval.

Callé, y la luz escuchó mi silencio.

In the slow elation of her thought I was a firefly, footsteps on an uncertain path.

And the wind in my heart beat,
a candle in a gale.

I was quiet, and the light attended to my silence.

Todo dolor tiene su momento. Verdades inquebrantables yo seguí en los pasos de los astros, la señal que desconoce el tiempo del alumbramiento y transcurre entre ambiguos deslaves. ¿Qué mano respira el aura de los cedros sin miedo a suceder? Tócame, oma mis brazos, flor a punto de derramar la elevación de su tallo.

> El hombre sólo es hombre, mientras tú, oh dulcísimo cáliz, vives en el imperio donde el velo del ángel se desgarra.

> *¡Almacenad los trigos para la hambruna, el remo vertical cuando el cierzo arrecia! Inclinados ante la ceniza imploramos la nuda semilla de la desvergüenza!*

Es un engaño el azar. ¿O es que la luz se apiada del pobre de corazón al ver su paso ciego en la colina? ¿Floreció o es eterna la caléndula, la tersa serenidad del quetzal?

> Horas en el transcurso infinito del árbol. Probé su sed, temblé ante la tempestad, la negación con su voluntad de poderío.

Acompáñame, sé mi guía en la piedad, alcánzame esa rosa que en tus labios se transforma en vino dulce. Ave, asciende la colina que mide las longitudes de mi origen. ¿No te das cuenta que tus ojos hablan el follaje? Ven, toma mi cuerpo, envuélveme de ternura cuando casi soy acacia. Oremos el largo beso en la pradera.

La estancia que visité en tu ausencia era una mariposa. La espina sangró savia azul. Te vi llegar en el sueño y una pluma flotó sembrando de alborozo los verdes portones del patio.

> Llegas entre gasas, colibrí.
> Tu perfume asigna tonalidades
> al paisaje y tiñe violácea la espesura.
>
> Llegaste por el inesperado camino
> limpiando de llaga mi leve sangre.

All pain has its instant. I followed relentless truths in the star trails, the gesture that ignores illumination's spell and elapses between confusing landslides. What hand touches the aura of cedars unafraid of their passing? Touch me, embrace the blooms of my arms cascading down my stem.

> Man is only man, while you, sweetest chalice,
> live in a realm where the angel's veil rips itself apart.

> *Store wheat for the famine, set the oar upright*
> *when the north wind swells! Leaning against ash*
> *we implore immodesty's bare seed!*

Fate is a trick. Or is light moved to pity the weak-hearted walking blindly on the hill? Did it flower, or is the marigold eternal, the quetzal's terse serenity?

> Hours in the infinite course of the tree. I tasted its thirst,
> trembled before tempest, negation, the power
>   of its will.

Join me. Be my guide in piety, proffer me that rose which on your lips becomes sweet wine. Bird, climb the hill that measures the longitudes of my lineage. Can't you see that your eyes speak to foliage? Come, take my body, wrap me in tenderness when I am almost acacia. We pray, a long kiss in the meadow.

The dwelling I visited in your absence was a butterfly. The spine bled blue sap. In my dream I saw you come back and a feather floated, spreading jouissance through the green patio gates.

> You come in gauze, hummingbird.
> Your perfume affixes tonalities
> to the landscape, stains violet the thicket.

> You came across the unexpected path
> cleansing the wound of my quiet blood.

II

RECORDACIÓN / REMINISCENCE

Creí con la creencia de los santos,
me pregunté
qué cosa es el amor.

¿Y la soledad y el dolor, esos pájaros nocturnos
que nos lanzan
a la hiriente
boca
de la hiena?

Amé creyendo en el abandono,
vi los cisnes dejar su estela,
el lago congelarse.

Vi encenderse
los lirios
bajo el fresno desnudo
desnuda yo
sobre la tarde.

Cuando miro la tarde todo se vuelve real.

I believed with the belief of the saints,
asked myself,
the meaning of love.

And solitude and pain, those nocturnal birds
that hurl us
to the hyena's
crushing
jaw?

I loved, submerged in abandonment,
saw the swans swirl their wake,
the lake freeze over.

I saw the iris
brighten
beneath the naked ash
naked myself
over the afternoon.

When I stare at the afternoon everything becomes real.

La memoria llena sus vacíos, los pájaros el cielo. Regresé a la rota mirada de la madre, sus frases oscuras, el vendaval manchaba la ropa en el patio, las hojuelas del hollín envolvían el durazno. El silbido de los trenes es recordación, sinceridad del árbol. Sólo la palabra restaura la quietud, allí donde la esencia afina su brillo.

>(Hablaste conmigo, escuché tu llanto, tus manos cerraron las fotografías. Miraste al suelo: "No abras la puerta, déjame estar sola." Mi padre encendió el televisor y se puso a mirarlo como quien mira un muro. Es diciembre: "No abras la puerta, di que no estoy." Una puerta abre otras puertas a lo mismo, me dije.)

Una llama alumbra los pasos, estorninos de inmensa geometría, su sangre en el lienzo vela lo blanco del espacio.

Entrar a la espesura no nos hace ciervos.

Memory fills its voids, birds the sky. I returned to my mother's shattered gaze, its dark phrases, a gale staining the bedding in the courtyard, flakes of soot shrouded the peach tree. The train whistle is reminiscence, a tree's sincerity. Only the word restores quietness, there where essence perfects its shimmer.

> (You spoke to me, I heard your lament, your hands covered the photographs. You looked down: "Don't open the door, leave me alone." My father turned on the TV and looked at it as if staring at a wall. December: "Never open the door. Say I'm not here." A door opens other doors leading us back, I said.)

A flame illuminates our steps, starlings of immense geometry, their blood on the canvas veils the whiteness of space.

Entering the thicket does not make us deer.

*¡**A**brid las puertas al mar, oh ángeles de mi karma, curad la llaga de este invierno! Santa Maria, madre di Dio, nostra è la carne degli angeli. Il mio corpo è più freddo dell'aria nebbiosa che sfiora la spiaggia.*

Esce dalla sfera il lamento dell'usignolo.

La tua esistenza
la tua sofferenza
sono il riflesso delle stelle
che affondano nell'acqua,
sono il canto dolente
dell'usignolo
quando si ferma l'albero.

Ed io vedo solo il tuo viso
tramontare
come il sole
della mia solitudine.

El ruiseñor presagia la altura de la tempestad.

*S*pread wide the doors to the sea, oh angels of my Karma. Cure this winter's wound! Holy Mary, madre di Dio, nostra è la carne degli angeli. Il mio corpo è più freddo dell'aria nebbiosa che sfiora la spiaggia.

Esce dalla sfera il lamento dell'usignolo.

La tua esistenza
la tua sofferenza
sono il riflesso delle stelle
che affondano nell'acqua,
sono il canto dolente
dell'usignolo
quando si ferma l'albero.

Ed io vedo solo il tuo viso
tramontare
come il sole
della mia solitudine.

The nightingale foretells the limit of the tempest.

Si es cierto que al crepúsculo todo tiene su hora, entonces vi un ánsar borrarse en la niebla, cegar las crestas el brillo, el águila perderse en su silencio, infinita.

El mar, el mar, don de nuestra falta. Y en el pretil, el jaspeado verdor del grillo. Oh Dios, abraza este cuerpo, es mi lengua, es el fluir de mi sangre entre olivos.

(Sus ojos miraron el principio, amaron la duración de la flor, pero el dolor cubrió el oro silencio de Sainápuchi.)

Arde en su soledad la piedra.

If it is true that at dusk everything follows its hour, then I glimpsed a duck erase itself in the fog, the ridges blinding the light, the eagle's silence dissolve in the infinite sky.

The sea, the sea, the grace of our absence. On the parapet, the cricket's mottled black. Oh God, embrace my body, it is my tongue, the stream of my blood among olive trees.

(Their eyes watched the beginning, loved the duration of the flower, but pain sheltered the gold silence of Sainápuchi.)

The stone burns in its solitude.

Piedra que en mi camino he dejado morir
—yo también fui piedra—,
el silencio como principio de su resonancia.
Y la palabra es llave
para alumbrar
el filo de lo que ya no es.

*pietra morta in pietra viva
in guisa d'uom pensi e pianga e scriva.*

Stone that I let die on my path
—I too was a stone—
silence like the beginning of its resonance.
And the word is key
to illuminate
the edge of what no longer is.

pietra morta in pietra viva
in guisa d'uom pensi e pianga e scriva.

III

EL ORDEN DEL MUNDO / THE ORDER OF THE WORLD

Mi madre me enseñó a caminar el desierto sin quemarme los pies. Ella, descalza en un ángulo de sol, extendió hasta mí su sombra de árbol enfermo.

Caí dos veces en la fuente del Parque Lerdo,
dos veces mi rostro
no encontró
la gracia de una herida.

Bajo delgada lama sentí el sosiego de dorados peces.
Ella cambió mi ropa
como quien presagia la doble caída.
No supe qué decir al escuchar
abrirse su aterrado silencio.

Espina del pez, forma labrada por el verbo.

¿Qué se busca? ¿Qué alcanza en su límite la llama?
Distancia es aquello que nunca sabremos decir.

My mother taught me how to walk barefoot across the desert without burning my feet. Barefoot in an angle of sunlight, she stretched out to me her shadow of a sick tree.

>
> Twice I fell in the Lerdo Park fountain,
> twice my face
> did not receive
> the grace of a wound.
>
> I felt the calm of golden fish beneath the thin moss.
> She changed my clothes
> like someone predicting a second fall.
> I didn't know what to say as I heard
> terror opening in her silence.

Fish spine, form carved by the verb.

What do we search for? What does the flame reach for in its limits? Distance is what we can never name.

Ven, déjame besar tus ojos, el alba derrama su niebla en el huerto, lee conmigo las páginas de una historia no contada, los pasos en la nieve, las manos de ternura que se desvanecen con las horas, tu lengua de arena disolviéndose en las dunas.

¡Oh, soledad, tú vaticinas!
¡Oh, espina del pez, traspasa mi silencio!

Come, let me kiss your eyes, dawn sheds its fog in the orchard.
Read with me the pages of an unwritten story, steps
in the snow, tender hands fading with the hours,
your words, like sand, dissolving on the dunes.

        Oh solitude, you portend!
        Oh fish spine, trespass my silence!

Ásperas sandalias fatigaron el desierto, la sed. Los leones azules me abrieron esa puerta. Y en el ámbar, la línea negra desdibujó mi destino.

¡Cuánto espanto confinado!
¡Cuánto olvido nuestra lengua!
Y el dolor, la mancha que impregna
el mármol, el aulos,
la veta rugosa del cedro.

(Al morir la tormenta atravesé las
inciertas arenas y alcé un muro
contra el cielo de Al Asad.)

Threadbare sandals exhausted the desert, thirst; blue lions opened that door for me. And in the amber, the black line misplaced my destiny.

       So much horror restrained!
       So much oblivion in our language!
       And pain, the stain imbuing
       marble, the aulos,
       the cedar's rough grain.

       (When the storm died I sailed across
       uncertain sands and raised a wall
       against the sky of Al Asad.)

No desaparece de mis ojos aquel cielo. Sueño aún tus pasos en el granito manchado de gris.

E la paura diventa pace nella dimenticanza. E il sogno diventa acqua se scoppia quella tenerezza che solo il tempo raggiunge; nella casa non c'era l'acquoso fiorire, non c'era la vita creata da quel Dio, neanche il rumore della smarrita solitudine.

Non ho mai visto quel viso rosso di cielo sconvolgersi, non ho mai visto quelle mani vellutate perdersi fra le colline, mai, non avevo mai sentito la musica della sua voce che mi chiamava, il richiamo della sua follia.

That sky does not fade from my eyes. I still dream of your steps on the stained gray granite.

E la paura diventa pace nella dimenticanza. E il sogno diventa acqua se scoppia quella tenerezza che solo il tempo raggiunge; nella casa non c'era l'acquoso fiorire, non c'era la vita creata da quel Dio, neanche il rumore della smarrita solitudine.

Non ho mai visto quel viso rosso di cielo sconvolgersi, non ho mai visto quelle mani vellutate perdersi fra le colline, mai, non avevo mai sentito la musica della sua voce che mi chiamava, il richiamo della sua follia.

Esa noche soñé tordos sin plumaje. Una enorme matriz rojo-violácea gelatinosa se desprendía de mi cuerpo, el pulpo y sus ventosas. Esa noche de multiformes ondulaciones el mar cedió al alumbramiento.

Elizabeth, lléveme contigo la marea,
que el viento borre nuestros rostros
nacidos de rocoso seno.

Quiero contemplar el monumento,
los riscos, la plata dispersa de la espuma.

De todos los silencios, prefiero el mar.

Lento se mece el sueño del agua.

That night I dreamed of featherless thrush. An enormous womb, red-violet, viscid, fell from my body, the octopus and its suckers. That night multiformed undulations, the sea succumbed
to illumination.

>   Elizabeth, let me walk with you along the shore,
>   the wind erases our faces
>   born from rocky breasts.
>
>   I want to contemplate the monument,
>   the cliffs, the foam's scattered silver.

Of all silence, I prefer the sea.

Slowly the sound of water sways.

Recorrí las veredas, escuché el llanto del venero, allí extravié el fondo de mi tempestad. ¿Dónde inicia el fin de la mirada? ¿Dónde se rompe el primer hilo de la cometa? Recordé la tierra sobre su rostro, las rosas calladas, en su pecho el misal. El deshilachado listón, el Salmo, y en mis ojos el torrente espumeante de las aguas.

El destino trazó lirios en el viento, jade de rota inscripción.
¿Y el hombre, ese vino derramado en la tierra?

El cielo se cubrió con una desgarrada tiniebla.
Palidecieron las agujas de los templos.
Se colmó de vacío la antigua memoria del pez.

I traveled over paths, heard a cry from the spring, and there I lost my tempest's core. Where does the end of one's gaze begin? Where does the first thread of the comet fray? I remembered dirt on her face, silent roses, the missal on her chest. The worn ribbon, the Psalm, and in my eyes torrential water foaming.

    Destiny traced lilies on the wind, jade of a broken inscription.
    And man, that wine spilled over the ground?

    The sky covered itself with tattered darkness.
    The temple spires faded.
    The ancient memory of fish filled with emptiness.

Se alzaba tu voz como una escalera
bajo el agua, era tu ausencia. / Olga Ayub,
¿qué hacías cada tarde en tu cuarto?
Te imaginaba tendida en el sofá,
la pila de periódicos,
la cortina corrida,
en tu vientre
los miedos
encerrados
como tú
tras esa
puerta
de cedro
que aún
no logro abrir.

(¿Existe una escalera que besa el agua, o es el fondo
de la arena ascendiendo turbia hacia lo real?)

Your voice reached like a ladder
under water, it was your absence. / Olga Ayub,
what did you do afternoons in your room?
I imagined you lying on the sofa,
the stack of newspapers,
the curtains drawn,
in your womb
your fears
locked up
like you
behind
a cedar
door
I still
cannot open.

(Is there a ladder that skims the water, or is it bottom
sand turbidly rising toward the real?)

Luego de mi muerte
nada quedará, no habrá
memoria mía.

Yo también yazgo sola,
sombra que en un solo fondo
se desparrama.

Lento paso del caimán.
Nostalgia
de ánsares
hacia el hueco inmenso del cielo.

Dije sed, y la playa se hizo plata.
Dije huerto y el olivo ardió.

After my death
nothing will remain, there will be
no memory of me.

I too lie alone,
a shadow spilling
into a single depth.

Slow pace of the caiman.
Longing
of geese
for the sky's immense hollow.

I said thirst, and the beach turned silver.
I said orchard and the olive tree burned.

Al silencio me abracé. Se astilló el brillo naranja del firmamento, los robles enmudecieron, la polilla se arremolinó en las farolas. El amor intangible de los amantes se disolvía en la lumbre. Vi fragmentos de espejo, su manantial incesante esmaltaba los pliegues del coral.

Esa tarde regresé a la albufera. Una inmensa soledad me miró. Vi el ave del desierto hundirse en el horizonte, el sol caer sobre los cedros, hundirse en mí la sombra. Mi cuerpo ascendió más allá de los tordos en la bruma.

Solo muere el arroyo.

I held silence. The firmament's orange glow ruptured, the oaks fell silent, moths swirled around the streetlamps. The intangible love of lovers dissolved in the flame. I saw mirror fragments, an ever-flowing spring varnished the coral pleats.

That evening I went back to the lagoon. An immense solitude looked at me. I saw the desert bird sink into the horizon, the sun fall over the cedars, the shadow sink into me. My body rose beyond the thrush in the mist.

The stream dies alone.

*Cuando te bajas de mi cuerpo
se agrietan la arena
y mi sed.*

When you climb off my body
the sand and my thirst
crack.

*¡**C**alma el ave en su elevación!*

¿Qué nombramos? ¿Qué imagen
de nuestro yo rescata el piélago?
Las nubes avanzan y el cielo persiste, inmóvil.
Mañana la luz arreciará invencible,
el tigre y su garra inmortal.
Y Dios hallará refugio en mi plegaria.

Orar, oírse en la incertidumbre.

Elevation calms the bird!

What do we name? What image
of ourselves does the open sea salvage?
The clouds move forward, and the sky persists, motionless.
Tomorrow light will intensify, invincible,
the tiger and its immortal paw.
And God will find refuge in my prayers.

Pray, hear yourself in the uncertain.

Nadie dice nada cuando muere el mar.
Nadie sabe que al llegar el día
nadie dirá nada de la luz.

              Sombras asomándose a la oscuridad.

Nada hay de cierto en el cielo.
Nada. Ni estas palabras.
Tal vez aquella mancha de gardenias junto al sabino,
el rojo horizonte al abrirse el final.

           En el comienzo sin final, el ave nace su destino.

No one says anything when the sea dies.
No one knows that when day comes
no one will say anything about light.

Shadows approaching darkness.

There is nothing certain in the sky.
Nothing. Not even these words.
Perhaps that cluster of gardenias beside the cypress,
the red horizon when the end opens.

In the endless beginning, the bird gives birth to its circumstance.

No todo es su decir. La melancolía en la habitación
es orilla silente,
latido prematuro.

No todo nos expulsa:
hay regiones que son sílabas de sombras.
No todo es nuestra lengua.

Not everything is what is said. Melancholy in the bedroom
is a noiseless shore,
a premature throb.

Not everything expels us:
there are regions that are syllables of shadows.
Not everything is our tongue.

IV

SOMOS LA HERIDA / WE ARE THE WOUND

Voz, eras el mar.

Y el descenso, la herida.
Te vi desde el ojo del buey, oh Niobe,
en tu negro aposento.
Tus manos sujetan
el raído eslabón,
llamándome.

Las flores negras del pantano
son voces de hojas caídas.
Todo lo oscuro,
toda la ruina
permanece.

Io voglio essere sfogliata dall'universo, trascinata dall'ombra che più non vede quell'immobile dolore dell'usignolo nel gelo. Siamo soltanto l'ombra del sogno, il ritorno al primo palpito. E io affondo nel desiderio di perdermi nella fessura dell'aria.

La piedra hablará un dolor que nadie escuchará.

Voice, you were the sea.

And descent, the wound.
Niobe, I saw you through the porthole
in your dark chamber.
Your hands hold
the frayed link,
calling me.

The black flowers from the swamp
are voices of fallen leaves.
All things dark,
all ruin
remains.

Io voglio essere sfogliata dall'universo, trascinata dall'ombra che più non vede quell'immobile dolore dell'usignolo nel gelo. Siamo soltanto l'ombra del sogno, il ritorno al primo palpito. E io affondo nel desiderio di perdermi nella fessura dell'aria.

The stone will speak of a pain no one will hear.

Y yo me hundo en el deseo de perderme,
en el estanque que me agita:
ser, dónde el ser.

Sólo el amor sostiene
la gravitación violeta
de los plumbagos.

Sol que a un tiempo
alivia y seca.

La mirada de la madre perdura
prolongación de una ausencia.

Fui a hablar mi sueño pero sólo escuché...
Salí deseando no haber mirado nunca.

I sink in the desire to lose myself,
in the lake that shifts me about:
being, where does my being abide?

Only love supports
the violet gravitation
of plumbagos.

Sun that both
soothes and scorches.

> *The mother's gaze endures*
> *the length of an absence.*
>
> *I wanted to speak of my dream but only heard…*
> *I left wishing I had never looked.*

Háblame de otra luz, la vasija está en el suelo.
Siento miedo al naufragio, al río de pájaros
entre las lápidas. Miedo, siempre miedo
a las campanadas que ciñen la isla.

Te sientas a mirar cardúmenes,
lirios giraban
por toda la habitación
llagándome.

De aquel muro la voz, las volutas,
el rostro de los muertos que amé.
Regresan como una fría
tarde en la banca solitaria del piano.

¡Nació allí el brillo de la tormenta!

Tell me about another light, the shard is on the ground.
I am afraid of the wreck. A river of birds
swerves around the grave stones. Fear, always fear
of the tolling bells crowning the island.

You sit and watch the shoals,
lilies twisting
around the room
wounding me.

From that wall the voice, scrolls,
the faces of the dead I loved.
They come back like dusk
chill on a solitary bench at the piano.

Over there, the storm's radiance came to life!

(El miedo disuelve el cuerpo del espejo,
ígneo abandono de ciega mirada rota.)

Madre, eras lumbre en mi fluir.

El agua lamía la luz del escollo.
Ardía la arena de aquel mar cuando los pájaros
enlutaron la casa.

La muerte de la niña
cuando el tren equivocó la vía.

(Fear dissolves the mirror's figure,
fiery abandonment in the empty gaze.)

Mother, you were a flame in my drifting.

Water licked the reef light.
Sand of that sea burned when the birds
mourned above the house.

The girl's death
when the train chose the wrong track.

V

UN ALTAR LA AUSENCIA /
AN ALTAR OF ABSENCE

Liel, la voz salía de la sábana. Su boca arrojaba llanto,
era el rostro del viento, era el rastro del reptil.
Liel, mueres cada noche en mí.

Liel, no eran espectros, el dolor era real,
escuché el estruendo en mis huesos,
un cuerpo despojado apenas de su carne.

Liel, ¿cómo se vuelve a los pliegues del origen,
cómo al tiempo cruel del desamparo, cómo, si el
rostro ha entrado ya en la tierra de la oscuridad?

Liel, the voice came out of the sheet. Its mouth spewed lament,
was the wind's face, was the reptile's wake.
Liel, each night you die inside me.

Liel, they were not shadows, the pain was real,
I heard the din in my bones,
a body hardly bereft of its skin.

Liel, how do I return to the creases of our origin,
like abandonment's cruel time, as if
my face had already entered the dark earth?

Una paloma entre nubes
y destellos de aguas quietas
busca sumergirse.

Oscura, se hunde en el silencio,
se desvanece entre los peces.

A dove between clouds
and flashes of calm waters
searches for immersion.

Dark, it sinks into silence,
it dissipates among the fish.

Mar, la niebla es tu silencio.
Mar, al risco arriban los vencejos.
Mar, meces interminable el nacer.

El vendaval dispersa lo que arropa del comienzo, el instante retrocede de transparencia en transparencia, huella la piedra, los claros de los olmos, los resquicios de lo inmóvil. Ese mismo trino engendra la alianza de quienes vuelven sin terminar el viaje, esa marea que nos lleva a la quietud-olvido, a la orilla donde mirasrestos de peces en la espuma.

Torrencial es la sequía.

Sea, the fog is your silence.
Sea, the swifts alight on the cliff.
Sea, you endlessly rock the dawn.

The gale scatters what it first covered, the instant recedes from clarity to clarity, tracks over the stone, the elm clearing, the gaps in the motionless. The same trill begets the bond between those returning without completing their journey, that tide that leads us to quiet/oblivion, to the shore where you watch the remains of fish in the surf.

The drought is torrential.

Esa tarde recorrí el jardín. Las hojas picadas del peral auguraban mala cosecha. Ya noche, atenta a las manecillas, entreví el brillo de la magnolia, sus henchidas venas como manos de madre que muestra el mapa a sus hijos. Sentada en la cama recordé sus ojos apagados, su mueca ante el espejo: la miraba mirarse, desconocer su rostro …morir de oscuridad.

Y la soñaba: eran tres palmas frente al mar, el rojo inaplazable del cielo, sus lentos pasos, y la tristeza, como una mancha de limón en el granito.

That afternoon I wandered around the garden. The punctured leaves on the pear tree presaged a meager harvest. Already night, attentive to the clock's small hands, I glimpsed the magnolia's glimmer, its swollen veins like a mother's hands showing a map to her children. Sitting on the bed I remembered her dull eyes, her grimace in the mirror: I watched her look at herself, not recognize her face…die from darkness.

My dream: three palm trees facing the sea, the sky's urgent red, her slow steps, and sadness, like a stain
of lemon on granite.

Apenas se oía el polvo,
latía la luz en los intersticios de la veneciana,
y tú esperabas la llegada de la galera.
Flotaba el brillo en el oleaje. Remos a la orilla.
¿Llegó, se fue la embarcación?
Casi todo resplandecía. Casi todo.

¿Por qué el sauce no reflejó la alberca?
El ave sí cantó, a pesar del vaticinio
callado viento de azafrán
habitaría esa noche la pradera.

Eras tú, entrando en la habitación, tú atravesando el aire.
Desnuda te esperé. La bañera rebosaba deseo,
el árbol inclinando, la humedad suave
del tacto, los azulejos, la luz
de la cerámica en los cuerpos.

Luego, el reposo la llama. Ciegos
nos hundimos en el lino,
roces que colman el abandono
cuando al hielo regresan los cisnes.

You could hardly hear the dust,
light pulsed through the venetian blinds,
and you waited for the galley to arrive.
Glitter floated on the waves. Oars on the shore.
Arrival, or was the ship leaving?
Almost everything glowed. Almost everything.

Why didn't the willow reflect the shallows?
Yes, a bird sang, despite the hushed
prophetic saffron wind
it would dwell in the night meadow.

It was you, entering the room, you traversing the air.
Naked I waited for you. The bath overflowed with desire,
the tree leaning, humid,
the tiles, their light
on our bodies.

Then, the flame's repose. Blind
we sank into the linen,
caresses that fill emptiness
when swans return to the ice.

Nieta eras de tu madre, y la noche, el tallo astillado del leatris.

Sólo si la espada es real se abre
el corazón al infortunio.

Un ábside de sol, y el viento dejó entrar
la soledad por todas las cuarteaduras.

(Liel, había miedo en su mirada.)
　　(Dios, ¿en dónde estabas a la hora de mi resurrección?)
　　　　(Y tú, ave del desierto, ¿en qué venero apagabas
　　　　　　tu canto?)

Granddaughter, you were your mother's, and the night, the splintered stem of the leatris.

Only if the sword is real can the heart receive misfortune.

An apse of sun: the wind bent under solitude and entered the fissures.

(Liel, her gaze filled with fear.)
(Lord, where were You the hour of my resurrection?)
(And you, desert bird, in what vein did you extinguish your song?)

Vetustas barcazas navegamos,
agua siempre infiel,
seca sangre aferrada
a esta rancia
melancolía.

                    Brillaba en el muro el reflejo del
río
                    bajo el puente donde los veleros,
los
                    picos de las gaviotas, guiaban vencidos
hálitos
                    de cedro, eco del viento,
como
                    una segunda señal, un grito
inaudible
                    en la torre,
cerco
                    de malaquita sacudido por leyes
sin
                    hombres que desde su trono de
lluvia
                    desvelarán el azar.

We sailed ancient barges,
the water always unfaithful,
dry blood clinging
to this rancid
melancholy.

                The river's reflection shimmered on the
wall
                beneath the bridge by the sailboats,
gull
                beaks, nodded defeated,
cedar
                breaths, wind echo,
as if
                a second signal, a cry
inaudible
                in the tower,
a malachite
                enclosure shaken by laws
without
                men who, from their throne of
rain
                unveiled fate.

Un dolor enciende el silencio, y en la habitación, el ánsar de la niebla. Húmedo mi cuerpo en la llama.

De nada suspendidos nombrar el amor buscamos.

Solo en su requiebro el mar.

(Ese día, Liel, me encontré en sus ojos: el sol caía en los tiestos, en el Libro, en la ceniza. El viento abrió mi sueño. Ese día, Liel, vi flotar su cuerpo sobre el solsticio del lago.)

Señor, yo soy falta.
Soy Tu falta.

Suffering ignites silence, a room like a goose flying out of the fog. Damp, my body in flame.

Name the love we search for, hanging in the void.

Alone in its enticement, the sea.

(That day, Liel, I found myself in his eyes: the sun fell on the flowerpots, on the Book, on the ash. The wind opened up my dream. That day, Liel, I saw his body float on the solstice of the lake.)

Lord, I am need.
I am Your need.

No debí haber nacido.

*Blanco fuego flotó ese día
en el brillo del marjal.*

Al alba escuchas el bastón del ciego
y no te atreves
a distinguir
la lumbre.

I wish I'd never been born.

*White fire floated that day
in the splendor of the moor.*

At dawn you listen to the blind man's cane
and you do not dare
isolate it
from the flame.

El Libro dice: crea la imagen única de la realidad.
Yo digo: crea la imagen de la ausencia.

The Book says: create the single image of reality.
I say: create the image of absence.

VI

NUESTRA DESCREENCIA / OUR DISBELIEF

Erotizo mis palabras
Porque no puedo
Erotizar mi cuerpo

Las lleno de color
De fruto
Al reventar

Erotizo lo que toco
Menos la carne
Pues es tan grande mi deseo

Que la carne
Si tocada
En agua ardería

Erotizo cada hoja
La tinta
El filo del cajón

Ardo en el teclado
El mouse
Lo oblicuo del bolígrafo

Erotizo mi voz
Mis senos contra el vidrio
La máscara del Buda en el buró

La pobre cruz de Cristo
Su sangre
Sus espinas

Después de todo
Nada es pasión
Sino madero irredento
Sólo un madero irredento

I eroticize my words
Because I cannot
Eroticize my body

I fill them with the color
Of fruit
When it bursts

I eroticize what I touch
Except for flesh
My desire is so great

Flesh
If touched
In water would burn

I eroticize each page
The ink
The edge of the drawer

I burn on the keyboard
The mouse
The pen's slant

I eroticize my voice
My breasts against glass
The Buddha mask in the bureau

Christ's poor cross
Its blood
Its thorns

After all
Nothing is passion
But an unalterable timber
Only an unalterable timber

María Shalhoup la llaman en el desierto, a donde huyó dejándonos su imperfecta miseria. Entonces, enjugó sus ojos en la sal.

Hablabas la lengua que te vio nacer en la estepa de Tell Brak. Vaciaste tu corazón. Entregaste tu sol a los sin ojos. ¡Cuánta iridiscencia en los alcázares! ¡Cuánto fulgor las escarpadas colinas de Duma! Reunidos en la casa unos a otros leían su indescifrable destino. Y ella, la que ardió, colmó con su leche la invertebrada higuera.

¡La plegaria será dicha!
¡Los poderosos confundirán el oro con los cuervos!
¡Lirios nacerán a las sábanas de quienes alcen su rostro en la borrasca!

Asciende la voz
desde una llama fría.

Ven a mis ojos, María,
en el orto de tu bendición.

They call her María Shalhoup in the desert, where she fled leaving us her imperfect misery. Then, she wiped her eyes with salt.

You spoke the language that watched your birth on the steppe of Tell Brak. You emptied your heart. You surrendered your sun to the eyeless. So much iridescence in the fortress! So much radiance on the steep hills of Duma! Gathered in the house they read their undecipherable destiny to one another. And she, the one who burned, showered the bent fig tree with milk.

The prayer will be joyous!
The mighty will mistake gold for ravens!
Lilies will be born on the sheets of those who raise their face in the tempest!

The voice rises
out of cold flame.

Come to my eyes, María,
in the sunrise of your blessing.

María, María, María: tus ojos guardan lo cenizo del olivo.
Acompáñame en mi ascenso hacia los ríos que de lo alto despeñan.

(Atravesé los diluvios del pacto sagrado, recorrí mi sed sin
más voz que el madrigal, mas tu cuerpo acmeico no retengo.
Eras blanca, María, entre las sábanas: de la lumbre ascendías
aromada de cedros. Te veo en las alturas de mi sangre,
junto al cesto de los peces.)

Sendero el ojo que se adentra en la corteza.

Fulgor de plata todas las soledades del amor,
temblor de vasijas lo oscuro,
lento vaciarse de huesos.

María, María, María: your eyes possess the olive tree's ash.
Join me in my ascent toward the rivers that flow down from above.

(I traversed the floods of the sacred covenant, my thirst wandered with no more voice than the madrigal, but I cannot hold your Acmeist body. You were white, María, between the sheets: you rose out of the cedar-scented light. I see you in the heights of my blood, next to the fish tubs.)

A path, the eye that penetrates tree bark.

All the solitudes of love glint silver,
the dark tremor of vases
a slow depletion of bones.

(Esa noche entré en comunión con el mar.
Caí al fondo de sus ojos y en el oleaje
espejo fue la incertidumbre.)

Bajo el granado un oleaje de humo blanco,
la sombra del arroyo,
la bendición del pan.
La quietud que sólo da una mancha de gardenias.
Para alumbrar
basta un breve recuento de pétalos.

        Oh, noche,
        arráncame de esta casa.
        Astillada llega a mí la claridad.

(That night I entered into communion with the sea. I fell into the depths of her eyes and in the surge uncertainty was a mirror.)

A wave of white smoke under the pomegranate,
the stream's shadow,
the bread's blessing.
The quiet that comes from a cluster of gardenias.
To illuminate
a brief account of petals.

>Night,
>pluck me from this house.
>Clarity comes to me splintered.

Nuestra mirada flota en el mar.
Nuestra mirada se hunde en el horizonte.
Nuestra mirada se cifra en el cuerpo de la sangre.

Cierra la noche la certeza oculta.
La guerra de los muertos prepara su festín
en altares de piedra.

Legiones bajan a sacrificar el orden de las bestias,
días en que el amor es sangre derramada,
oscuras estancias vacías

Our gaze floats on the sea.
Our gaze sinks into the horizon.
Our gaze is reduced to the body of blood.

Night obstructs the certainty of day.
The war of the dead prepares its feast
on stone altars.

Legions come down to sacrifice the order of beasts,
days in which love is spilled blood,
empty, dark dwellings.

Dicen los santos que el descenso es la herida,
que las confesiones mejores son las más dolorosas,
que el deseo seca la necesidad.

        Y yo me buscaba en el agua,
        y me perdía entre los sepias
        tallos del laurel.

                Pero tú fundas el silencio,
                y esparces la lluvia.
                Madre, no acabo nunca de nombrarte.

The saints say that descent is a wound,
that the best confessions are the most painful,
that denial dries up desire.

        I looked for myself in the water,
        and lost myself among the sepia
        laurel stems.

                But you endow silence,
                and scatter the rain.
                Mother, I never stop naming you.

¿Atravesaré el lago,
el fango entre las piedras?
No hay reflejo de luna, no hay espacio en su agua.

El trisar de las aves migrando.
El árbol caído.
Y, tierra, la sed.

¡Flor, soy el ojo de tu sangre!

Will I cross the lake,
the mire between rocks?
There is no moon reflection, there is no space in its water.

The fracture of migrating birds.
The fallen tree.
And, soil, the thirst.

Flower, I am the eye of your blood!

MYSTERIUM TERRAE

Surqué la flor, la tempestad en la carne del árbol,
y el mar se abrió a la posibilidad.

    Lumen Dei non videmus
    Lumini Dei non credemus

        (Cáliz la desmoronada palabra,
        aromadas hojas de guindo
        tus manos cuando lavan los jades.)

El alba derrama su niebla,
y tú cierras mi desnudez.

I notched the flower, the tempest in the tree's flesh,
and the sea unlocked possibility.

    Lumen Dei non videmus
    Lumini Dei non credemus

        (Chalice, the eroded word,
        scented cherry leaves
        your hands when they burnish jade.)

            Dawn scatters its fog,
            and you confine my nakedness.

Tu vedi la mia anima solo quando è ombrosa
Tu credi nella mia anima solo se fiorisce dolente

Agnus Dei, tu scateni le tempeste
Agnus Dei, tu non togli questo smarrimento

Mysterium lucis necessitas verbum inveniendi est.

Tu vedi la mia anima solo quando è ombrosa
Tu credi nella mia anima solo se fiorisce dolente

Agnus Dei, tu scateni le tempeste
Agnus Dei, tu non togli questo smarrimento

Mysterium lucis necessitas verbum inveniendi est.

*Ese calvario es el mar de sombras
abriéndose desde la llaga.*

Azufradas olas entregan su último hálito.

*That agony is a sea of shadows
opening itself from the wound.*

Sulfurous waves deliver their last breath.

Y cuando llegue la noche el reposo entrará en mi alma.

Estás triste en el exilio y la hermosura
Nada puede
En la más dulce de las iras
En la más infiel de las historias.

Cierra la noche la certeza del día
La guerra de los muertos prepara su festín
En un trono de piedra
Legiones bajan a sacrificar el orden de las bestias
Días en que el amor es sangre derramada
Oscuras estancias vacías.

Exclamación   fantasmas   hombres
De sílaba perfecta y puntos suspensivos
Aguardan la hora del comienzo
El puerto donde la muerte rompe las cadenas
Reconoce el balbucir
Y no se atreve a distinguir de nuevo
La lumbre.

When night arrives calm will enter my soul.

You are sad in exile and nothing
Becomes beauty
In sweet rage
In the most unfaithful stories.

Night closes day's certainty
The war of the dead prepares its feast
On a rock throne
Legions descend to sacrifice the arrangement of beasts
Days in which love is shed blood
Empty, dark dwellings.

Exclamation   ghosts   men
Out of perfect syllables and ellipses
They wait for the beginning
The port where death breaks chains
Recognizes the babble
And does not dare to classify
The light.

Elegiré la más fina y delgada como senda de mi confesión.
Escribiré el signo, apoyaré el pie derecho sobre la raíz,
y el ojo refulgirá, infinito.
Renacerá de tus manos el orto
y tú,
       serás fiel oyente del follaje.

I will select the most delicate, thinnest for the path to my confession.
I will write the sign, rest my right foot on the root,
and my eye will gleam, infinite.
From your hands the rising sun will be revived
and you,
       you will be the leaves' faithful listener.

Notes

The following works were read by Clariond during the composition of the poems:

DUSK: *The Complete Poems of Emily Dickinson*, Thomas H. Johnson, ed.

REMINISCENCE: Francesco Petrarch, Canzone II, de Canzoniere.

THE ORDER OF THE WORLD: From Sapho, *Poems and Fragments* (versions by Carlos Montemayor and Anne Carson).

WE ARE THE WOUND: Edmond Jabès, *El libro de las preguntas*, V. I y II, Ed. Siruela, Madrid, 1990.

AN ALTAR OF ABSENCE: From Néstor Braunstein, *Memoria y Espanto. Recuerdos de infancia.* Ed. Siglo XXI, México, 2009.

OUR DISBELIEF: Charles Wright, *Zodiaco negro* [*Black Zodiac*], Ed. Pretextos, 2002; *Una breve historia de la sombra* [*A Short History of the Shadow*], Ed. DVD, 2009.

MYSTERIUM TERRAE: Alda Merini, *Cuerpo de amor: un encuentro con Jesús*, Ed. Vaso Roto, Barcelona, 2008.

The following are first lines of poems where greater clarification may be needed:

"Lost, I watched the afternoon against the naked wind"
—The poet is addressing Emily Dickinson in this poem.

"From silence I needed, like death seeks a spark from the flower bloom"
—Throughout the text the multiple and distinct voices inside the poet reveal themselves: these are voices that gather breath from the translation of other poets. In this instance, Clariond has written the Latin, *That which is not miserably dying is not entirely dying*; it suggests an echo not only of the poet's multilingual experience, but also her ceaseless work as a translator. It should also be noted that I have chosen to

leave this and other sections untranslated, as they appear in the original Spanish text, in order to provide a similar reading experience as one might have when reading the original Spanish. Unless otherwise noted, all translations are mine.

"Spread wide the doors to the sea, oh angels of my Karma"
—In this Italian segment, the poet begins with a prayer, which evolves out of a practice common in this collection and the poet's other works, that of drawing substantial allusive weight from a subject and transferring it to the language of lament, of loss in yet another language. Here she begins with a gesture toward the beginning of T.S. Eliot's *The Waste Land*. She is also indicating that, like so many poets before her traveled abroad and made translation part of their writing practice, including W.S. Merwin and Charles Wright, two poets she also translates, multiple languages always reside in her. Clariond has spent more than twenty years translating the works of Alda Merini. She has said that Merini's voice is often present when she writes, and the language of that voice also entered into the composition of many of these poems.

> Mother of God, ours is the flesh
> of angels. My body is colder than the mist
> that hugs the beach.
>
> The nightingale's lament comes out of the sphere.
>
> Your being
> your suffering
> are the reflections of the stars
> that sink into the water
> they are the raw song
> of the nightingale
> when the tree is still.
>
> And I see your air
> set
> like the sun
> of my solitude.

"If it is true that at dusk everything follows its hour, then I"
—The beginning of this poem is in response to the lines "Since then, at an uncertain hour, / That agony returns; / And till my ghastly tale is told, / This heart within me burns" in Coleridge's "The Rime of the Ancient Mariner." Sainápuchi was an Apache settlement and refuge in the Cuauhtémoc region of Chihuahua Mexico now mostly populated by Mennonite farmers.

"Stone that I let die on my path"
—From Petrarch's *Canzoniere*, "dead stone inside the living stone / in the form of a man, you think and mourn and write."

"Threadbare sandals exhausted the desert"
—Al Asad is in Iraq.

"That sky does not fade from my eyes"
—This is the poet's own poem, written in Italian:

> Fear becomes peace in forgetfulness.
> And dreams become water if they burst that tenderness
> only time can reach, in the house with no watery blooming,
> there was no life created by that God, nor was there a murmur
> of God's misplaced solitude.
>
> I have never seen that red face of the sky scowl, I have never
> seen those velvety hands lose themselves among the hills, never,
> never had I heard the music of the voice that called me,
> the call of madness.

"Your voice reached like a ladder"
—Olga Ayub is the poet's mother

"Voice, you were the sea."
—In Greek mythology, Niobe is described as a woman who compares herself to a goddess. She has the audacity to boast that she herself has given birth to twelve children (six boys and six girls), while the goddess Leto only bore two (the god Apollo and the goddess Artemis). Leto is offended by Niobe's hubris and sends her two children to punish her. Niobe, devastated when her children were killed, wept for days and finally turned into a stone that stands on Mt. Sipylon. In Ovid's version of the story, Niobe is not only turned into a stone, but this stone actually sheds tears. Again, this is the poet's own poem, written in Italian:

> I want to be riffled by the universe, dragged from the shadow blind
> to the motionless pain of a nightingale under frost. We are only
> the shadow of a dream, the return to the first heartbeat. And I sink
> in desire to lose myself in a sliver of air.

"Liel, the voice came out of the sheet."
— The use of Liel throughout this text is an allusion to William Blake's visions. The tone is of supplication explanation, as if the poet were articulating something with an immense need to be heard.

"They call her María Shalhoup in the desert"
>—María Shalhoup was the poet's grandmother. The poet is interested in alluding to a relationship between her grandmother and the Virgin Mary; she uses "white" figures, for connotations of absence.

>When her grandmother was nine years old she was sent by boat to Mexico so she could keep house for her two older brothers. They married her to a man more than twice her age when she was 14. She had a son who, when he was 21, was institutionalized in a psychiatric hospital in Kirville, Texas, though the two of them were confined with the criminally insane before that. Afterwards she had six daughters. They lived in the Mexican state of Chihuahua, but when Pancho Villa came to power he expelled the Arab and Chinese populations from the Chihuahua region and they went to El Paso to live; it was here where the three youngest daughters were born. All of them were educated in English. That is, they were doubly exiled and grew up with two essential fears: exile and insanity, because when her son Jorge was institutionalized María Shalhoup also went insane. The poet's aunt, Jeannette, was schizophrenic. In the poet's house there was much illness and emotional pain, but there was also love.

>Tell Brak was an ancient city situated in North East Syria. Originally it was a center for royalty in the north of Mesopotamia.

>Duma is a small town in the north of Lebanon where María Shalhoup, the poet's grandmother, was born.

"I notched the flower, the tempest in the tree's flesh"
>—This is the poet's own poem, written in Latin:

>>We do not see the light of God
>>We will not have faith in the light of God.

"Tu vedi la mia anima solo quando è ombrosa"
>—This is the poet's own poem, written in Italian and Latin, intended to allude to the passage of night, that darkness has passed and day is opening up, that the wound is closing and the body, the self is beginning to heal:

>>You see my soul only when it is in shadow
>>You believe in my soul only in its sorrowful bloom

>>*Lamb of God*, you unleash the tempests
>>*Lamb of God*, you do not take away this loss
>>The word's mysterious light is an invention.

About the Poet

Jeannette L. Clariond (Chihuahua, Mexico, 1949) grew up between languages, which influenced how she looks at the world, her vision of reality and her poetics. A prolific poet and translator, she has won numerous awards and prizes for her poetry collections, including the Premio Nacional de Poesía Efraín Huerta for the collection *Deserted Memory*; the Premio Nacional de Poesía Gonzalo Rojas for *Everything Before Nightfall*; her book *Woman Turning Her Back* was a finalist for the Premio Nacional de Poesía Ramón López Velarde; and *Image of Silence* was a finalist for the Premio Cope in Peru. In addition to her poetry, Ms. Clariond has translated more than twenty books of poetry by American and European authors, including Charles Wright, Primo Levi, Elizabeth Bishop and Anne Carson. Over the last twenty five years she has translated ten books by the Italian poet Alda Merini. In 2002 Ms. Clariond received a Conaculta Rockefeller Foundation grant for her translation of Charles Wright's *Black Zodiac*, and from 2000 to 2006 she worked with the acclaimed critic, Harold Bloom, at Yale University. During this time, she translated important poetic works from the United States and co-edited and subsequently published the anthology, *The School of Wallace Stevens: A Profile of Contemporary North American Poetry*; the book was awarded the Latino Book Award's Best Translation Prize in 2013. Ms. Clariond is a collaborating member of the North American Academy of the Spanish Language, which has branches in Washington and New York. She is currently translating Anne Carson's book *Nox* into Spanish.

About the Translator

Curtis Bauer is the author of two poetry collections: *Fence Line* (BkMk Press, 2004) won the John Ciardi Poetry Prize; and *The Real Cause for Your Absence* was published by C&R Press in 2013. His translations include: *Eros Is More* (Alice James Books, 2014), by Juan Antonio González Iglesias; *From Behind What Landscape* (Vaso Roto Editions, 2015), by Luis Muñoz; and *Baghdad and Other Poems* (Poets@Work, 2015), by Jorge Gimeno. His poems and translations have appeared in the *Southern Review*, *The Indiana Review*, *The Literary Review*, and *The American Poetry Review*, among others. He is the publisher and editor of Q Avenue Press Chapbooks and the Translations Editor for *Waxwing Literary Journal*. He teaches Creative Writing, Comparative Literature, and Letterpress Printing at Texas Tech University.

About The Word Works

Since its founding in 1974, The Word Works has steadily published volumes of contemporary poetry and presented public programs. Its imprints include The Washington Prize, The Tenth Gate Prize, The Hilary Tham Capital Collection, and International Editions.

Monthly, The Word Works offers free literary programs in the Chevy Chase, MD, Café Muse series, and each summer it holds free poetry programs in Washington, D.C.'s Rock Creek Park. Word Works programs have included "In the Shadow of the Capitol," a symposium and archival project on the African American intellectual community in segregated Washington, D.C.; the Gunston Arts Center Poetry Series; the Poet Editor panel discussions at The Writer's Center; and Master Class workshops, and a writing retreat in Tuscany, Italy.

As a 501(c)3 organization, The Word Works has received awards from the National Endowment for the Arts, the National Endowment for the Humanities, the D.C. Commission on the Arts & Humanities, the Witter Bynner Foundation, Poets & Writers, The Writer's Center, Bell Atlantic, the David G. Taft Foundation, and others, including many generous private patrons.

An archive of artistic and administrative materials in the Washington Writing Archive housed in the George Washington University Gelman Library. It is a member of the Community of Literary Magazines and Presses and its books are distributed by Small Press Distribution.

wordworksbooks.org

INTERNATIONAL EDITIONS

Kajal Ahmad (Alana Marie Levinson-LaBrosse, Mewan Nahro
    Said Sofi, and Darya Abdul-Karim Ali Najin, trans., with
    Barbara Goldberg), *Handful of Salt*
Keyne Cheshire (trans.), *Murder at Jagged Rock: A Tragedy by Sophocles*
Jean Cocteau (Mary-Sherman Willis, trans.), *Grace Notes*
Yoko Danno & James C. Hopkins, *The Blue Door*
Moshe Dor, Barbara Goldberg, Giora Leshem, eds., *The Stones Remember:
    Native Israeli Poets*
Moshe Dor (Barbara Goldberg, trans.), *Scorched by the Sun*
Lee Sang (Myong-Hee Kim, trans.), *Crow's Eye View: The Infamy of Lee
    Sang, Korean Poet*
Vladimir Levchev (Henry Taylor, trans.), *Black Book of the Endangered Species*

THE TENTH GATE PRIZE

Jennifer Barber, *Works on Paper*, 2015
Lisa Lewis, *Taxonomy of the Missing*, 2017
Roger Sedarat, *Haji As Puppet*, 2016
Lisa Sewell, *Impossible Object*, 2014

THE WASHINGTON PRIZE

Nathalie Anderson, *Following Fred Astaire*, 1998
Michael Atkinson, *One Hundred Children Waiting for a Train*, 2001
Molly Bashaw, *The Whole Field Still Moving Inside It*, 2013
Carrie Bennett, *biography of water*, 2004
Peter Blair, *Last Heat*, 1999
John Bradley, *Love-in-Idleness: The Poetry of Roberto Zingarello*, 1995, 2ND edition 2014
Christopher Bursk, *The Way Water Rubs Stone*, 1988
Richard Carr, *Ace*, 2008
Jamison Crabtree, *Rel[AM]ent*, 2014
Jessica Cuello, *Hunt*, 2016
Barbara Duffey, *Simple Machines*, 2015
B. K. Fischer, *St. Rage's Vault*, 2012
Linda Lee Harper, *Toward Desire*, 1995
Ann Rae Jonas, *A Diamond Is Hard But Not Tough*, 1997
Susan Lewis, *Zoom*, 2017
Frannie Lindsay, *Mayweed*, 2009
Richard Lyons, *Fleur Carnivore*, 2005
Elaine Magarrell, *Blameless Lives*, 1991
Fred Marchant, *Tipping Point*, 1993, 2ND edition 2013
Ron Mohring, *Survivable World*, 2003
Barbara Moore, *Farewell to the Body*, 1990
Brad Richard, *Motion Studies*, 2010
Jay Rogoff, *The Cutoff*, 1994
Prartho Sereno, *Call from Paris*, 2007, 2ND edition 2013
Enid Shomer, *Stalking the Florida Panther*, 1987
John Surowiecki, *The Hat City After Men Stopped Wearing Hats*, 2006
Miles Waggener, *Phoenix Suites*, 2002
Charlotte Warren, *Gandhi's Lap*, 2000
Mike White, *How to Make a Bird with Two Hands*, 2011
Nancy White, *Sun, Moon, Salt*, 1992, 2ND edition 2010
George Young, *Spinoza's Mouse*, 1996

THE HILARY THAM CAPITAL COLLECTION

Nathalie Anderson, *Stain*
Mel Belin, *Flesh That Was Chrysalis*
Carrie Bennett, *The Land Is a Painted Thing*
Doris Brody, *Judging the Distance*
Sarah Browning, *Whiskey in the Garden of Eden*
Grace Cavalieri, *Pinecrest Rest Haven*
Cheryl Clarke, *By My Precise Haircut*
Christopher Conlon, *Gilbert and Garbo in Love*
    & *Mary Falls: Requiem for Mrs. Surratt*
Donna Denizé, *Broken like Job*
W. Perry Epes, *Nothing Happened*
David Eye, *Seed*
Bernadette Geyer, *The Scabbard of Her Throat*
Barbara G. S. Hagerty, *Twinzilla*
James Hopkins, *Eight Pale Women*
Donald Illich, *Chance Bodies*
Brandon Johnson, *Love's Skin*
Thomas March, *Aftermath*
Marilyn McCabe, *Perpetual Motion*
Judith McCombs, *The Habit of Fire*
James McEwen, *Snake Country*
Miles David Moore, *The Bears of Paris*
    & *Rollercoaster*
Kathi Morrison-Taylor, *By the Nest*
Tera Vale Ragan, *Reading the Ground*
Michael Shaffner, *The Good Opinion of Squirrels*
Maria Terrone, *The Bodies We Were Loaned*
Hilary Tham, *Bad Names for Women*
    & *Counting*
Barbara Ungar, *Charlotte Brontë, You Ruined My Life*
    & *Immortal Medusa*
Jonathan Vaile, *Blue Cowboy*
Rosemary Winslow, *Green Bodies*
Michele Wolf, *Immersion*
Joe Zealberg, *Covalence*

OTHER WORD WORKS BOOKS

Annik Adey-Babinski, *Okay Cool No Smoking Love Pony*
Karren L. Alenier, *Wandering on the Outside*
Karren L. Alenier, ed., *Whose Woods These Are*
Karren L. Alenier & Miles David Moore, eds.,
    Winners: A Retrospective of the Washington Prize
Christopher Bursk, ed., *Cool Fire*
Willa Carroll, *Nerve Chorus*
Grace Cavalieri, *Creature Comforts*
Abby Chew, *A Bear Approaches from the Sky*
Barbara Goldberg, *Berta Broadfoot and Pepin the Short*
Akua Lezli Hope, *Them Gone*
Frannie Lindsay, *If Mercy*
Elaine Maggarrell, *The Madness of Chefs*
Marilyn McCabe, *Glass Factory*
Kevin McLellan, *Ornitheology*
JoAnne McFarland, *Identifying the Body*
Leslie McGrath, *Feminists Are Passing from Our Lives*
Ann Pelletier, *Letter That Never*
Ayaz Pirani, *Happy You Are Here*
W.T. Pfefferle, *My Coolest Shirt*
Jacklyn Potter, Dwaine Rieves, Gary Stein, eds.,
    Cabin Fever: Poets at Joaquin Miller's Cabin
Robert Sargent, *Aspects of a Southern Story*
    & *A Woman from Memphis*
Miles Waggener, *Superstition Freeway*
Fritz Ward, *Tsunami Diorama*
Amber West, *Hen & God*
Nancy White, ed., *Word for Word*

www.ingramcontent.com/pod-product-compliance
Lightning Source LLC
Chambersburg PA
CBHW031334160426
43196CB00007B/682